Collins English I

G000155805

Amazing Leaders

Level 1
CEF A2

Text by
Silvia Tiberio

Series edited by
Fiona MacKenzie

Collins

HarperCollins Publishers
77–85 Fulham Palace Road
Hammersmith London W6 8JB

10 9 8 7 6 5 4 3 2 1

Original text
© The Amazing People Club Ltd

Adapted text
© HarperCollins Publishers Ltd 2014

ISBN: 978-0-00-754492-9

Collins® is a registered trademark of
HarperCollins Publishers Limited

www.collinselt.com

A catalogue record for this book is available
from the British Library

Printed in the UK by Martins the Printers

HarperCollins does not warrant that
www.collinselt.com or any other website
mentioned in this title will be provided
uninterrupted, that any website will be
error free, that defects will be corrected, or
that the website or the server that makes it
available are free of viruses or bugs. For full
terms and conditions please refer to the site
terms provided on the website.

These readers are based on original texts
(BioViews®) published by The Amazing
People Club group.® BioViews® and The
Amazing People Club® are registered
trademarks and represent the views of the
author.

BioViews® are scripted virtual interview
based on research about a person's life and
times. As in any story, the words are only
an interpretation of what the individuals
mentioned in the BioViews® could have
said. Although the interpretations are
based on available research, they do not
purport to represent the actual views of
the people mentioned. The interpretations
are made in good faith, recognizing that
other interpretations could also be made.
The author and publisher disclaim any
responsibility from any action that readers
take regarding the BioViews® for educational
or other purposes. Any use of the BioViews®
materials is the sole responsibility of the
reader and should be supported by their own
independent research.

Cover image © DNY59/istockphoto

MIX
Paper from
responsible sources
FSC **FSC™ C007454**
www.fsc.org

FSC™ is a non-profit international organisation established to promote the
responsible management of the world's forests. Products carrying the FSC
label are independently certified to assure consumers that they come from
forests that are managed to meet the social, economic and ecological needs
of present and future generations, and other controlled sources.

Find out more about HarperCollins and the environment at
www.harpercollins.co.uk/green

◆ CONTENTS ◆

Collins Amazing People Readers are collections of short stories. Each book presents the life story of five or six people whose lives and achievements have made a difference to our world today. The stories are carefully graded to ensure that you, the reader, will both enjoy and benefit from your reading experience.

You can choose to enjoy the book from start to finish or to dip in to your favourite story straight away. Each story is entirely independent.

After every story a short timeline brings together the most important events in each person's life into one short report. The timeline is a useful tool for revision purposes.

Words which are above the required reading level are underlined the first time they appear in each story. All underlined words are defined in the glossary at the back of the book. Levels 1 and 2 take their definitions from the *Collins COBUILD Essential English Dictionary* and levels 3 and 4 from the *Collins COBUILD Advanced English Dictionary.*

To support both teachers and learners, additional materials are available online at www.collinselt.com/readers.

The Amazing People Club®

Collins Amazing People Readers are adaptations of original texts published by The Amazing People Club. The Amazing People Club is an educational publishing house. It was founded in 2006 by educational psychologist and management leader Dr Charles Margerison and publishes books, eBooks, audio books, iBooks and video content which bring readers 'face to face' with many of the world's most inspiring and influential characters from the fields of art, science, music, politics, medicine and business.

◆ THE GRADING SCHEME ◆

The Collins COBUILD Grading Scheme has been created using the most up-to-date language usage information available today. Each level is guided by a brand new comprehensive grammar and vocabulary framework, ensuring that the series will perfectly match readers' abilities.

		CEF band	Pages	Word count	Headwords
Level 1	elementary	A2	64	5,000–8,000	approx. 700
Level 2	pre-intermediate	A2–B1	80	8,000–11,000	approx. 900
Level 3	intermediate	B1	96	11,000–15,000	approx. 1,100
Level 4	upper intermediate	B2	112	15,000–18,000	approx. 1,700

For more information on the Collins COBUILD Grading Scheme, including a full list of the grammar structures found at each level, go to www.collinselt.com/readers/gradingscheme.

Also available online: Make sure that you are reading at the right level by checking your level on our website (www.collinselt.com/readers/levelcheck).

William the Conqueror

◆ ◆ ◆

*c.*1027–1087

the first Norman King of England

I was 8 years old when my father died. My life was in danger and I had to learn to fight. When I <u>invaded</u> England, I was a very brave man. I <u>conquered</u> the whole country and kept it safe from attacks.

◆ ◆ ◆

I was from Normandy in the north of France and my father was the Duke of Normandy. When my father died in 1035, the <u>barons</u> of Normandy didn't want me to <u>rule</u> because I was only 8 years old. Many barons wanted to kill me. For ten years, my life was in danger. Finally, in 1045, I began to rule Normandy with the help of some <u>priests</u>.

But a lot of barons were still against me. In 1047, a group of them tried to <u>capture</u> me, but I was able to escape during the night. I rode my horse to Poissy to meet King Henry the First of France. 'A <u>rebellion</u> against me will be the start of a rebellion against you,' I said. The King's <u>army</u> helped me to fight. We won a <u>battle</u> against the barons. After that, I fought many other battles. I conquered more land and I had a big army of soldiers.

I visited England and met King Edward. He had a lot of enemies – people who fought against him – and I had a strong army, so I offered him my help. He didn't have any children, so he offered me the English <u>throne</u> <u>in return</u> for my help.

I also met Harold of Wessex, an English <u>nobleman</u>, who was captured in France. I talked to the King of France and asked him to <u>free</u> Harold. Then I met Harold and told him, 'King Edward promised me the English throne.' Harold was happy because he was free. He said, 'I'll help you to become King.' But when King Edward died on 5th January 1066, Harold broke his promise and named himself King. I was surprised. I was Norman, but the English throne was mine!

◆ ◆ ◆

Now it was time to prepare for another fight. I wanted to invade England and I had to plan my attack. I spent a lot of money on hundreds of new ships. I also <u>trained</u> a very large army of soldiers. In September 1066, my ships and soldiers were ready. We sailed across the English Channel on 27th September. The waves were high, but the winds were blowing in the right direction. It was a very dangerous journey and we arrived at Pevensey Bay in the south of England on 28th September.

When we arrived in England, King Harold and his army were in the north. They were fighting other battles there. The King had other enemies – other people wanted the English throne too!

We got off our ships and waited. While King Harold and his army were quickly <u>marching</u> south, we were having a good rest. When the King arrived at Hastings to fight against us, many of his soldiers were tired and <u>injured</u>. After a good rest, my soldiers and I were strong, healthy and ready for battle.

It was 14th October 1066. King Harold and his army were in a better position because they were at the top of a hill. But they made a mistake when they decided to come down the hill to fight. Soon, we were in <u>control</u> and King Harold was killed. I became the new King of England on 25th December 1066.

◆ ◆ ◆

My new job wasn't easy. I wasn't very popular among the English people and I had to stop several small rebellions. And I still had to conquer the rest of the country.

First, I took control of Dover, a <u>port</u> in the south, and London. I decided to rule England from London. I needed a castle to protect my position, so we began to build The Tower of London. Then, I asked my brothers to rule my new land and I went back to Normandy to see my family.

When I returned to England, I conquered the west and then, the north. In 1072, the whole country was mine!

Soon there was a new way of life in England. There were Norman <u>laws</u> and there was a new language – French. The Normans became the <u>rulers</u>. I gave them lands, and the English people worked in their lands. I built a lot of castles across the country. I needed them to protect the country against <u>invaders</u>. I also asked my people to collect information on the number of people in England and the farms and animals that they had. All this information was written in the *Domesday Book* in 1085.

I died in Normandy in 1087. The next two Kings of England, William the Second and Henry the First, were my sons.

The Life of William the Conqueror

*c.*1027 William was born in Normandy, France. He was the son of the Duke of Normandy.

1035 His father died. He became the Duke of Normandy. He was 8 years old.

1045 He began to rule Normandy with the help of some priests.

1053 He married Matilda of Flanders. They later had around nine children.

1064 King Edward promised him the English throne.

1066 King Edward died. Harold of Essex became King. William decided to invade England. William and Harold's armies met in the Battle of Hastings. King Harold was killed and William became King of England.

1067 He asked his brothers to rule England and returned to Normandy.

1068 Matilda became Queen of England.

1069 The King of Denmark invaded England. William stopped the invasion.

1071 William stopped a local rebellion.

1072 William invaded Scotland.

1083   William's wife became ill and died.

1085   William collected information about the
        people and places in England. It was written
        in the *Domesday Book*. It's the oldest legal
        document in Britain.

1087   William died in France. He was 60 years old.

Saladin

◆ ◆

1137–1193

the Muslim leader who fought against the Crusaders

I never lived in times of <u>peace</u>. In my land, there were <u>battles</u> during the whole of my life. I became a good soldier and the leader of a large <u>army</u>. I fought against the <u>Crusaders</u> and a lot of enemy <u>tribes</u>.

◆ ◆ ◆

I was born in the city of Tikrit, in Iraq. I was the son of a rich <u>Muslim</u> leader. When I was a child, I lived in Syria.

My parents and grandparents told me about the first <u>Crusade</u> – a war between Christians and Muslims. It was from 1096 to 1099. The Christians, who called themselves Crusaders, <u>invaded</u> our land to take <u>control</u> of the city of Jerusalem. Our people lost the war and it was a terrible time. Our houses were <u>destroyed</u> and a lot of people died.

When I was 8 years old, the Crusaders attacked us for the second time. I saw a lot of people die. They fought for control of the city of Jerusalem, We fought to protect our land, our families and our way of life.

My parents told me the stories of our tribe. I learnt how to read and write, and I also learnt to ride horses. I wanted to be a great horse rider. If I could ride a horse, I could save my life. Soldiers fought battles on horses, and battles were part of our life. We didn't only fight the Crusaders. We also fought enemy tribes.

When I was a young man, I met the oldest men of my tribe. They talked to me about the past. 'They're thinking about the wrong things,' I thought. 'We have to think about the future. We don't have to talk. We have to fight and attack.'

I decided to become a good soldier to protect my culture. I also decided to become the leader of the Muslim army against the Crusaders. I needed to meet the strongest soldiers of my time.

I went to the city of Damascus and I joined my uncle's army. His name was Shirkuh and he was a great leader. I became a good soldier with him. When one day, my uncle died at a party, I became the new leader of his army.

For the next 15 years, I fought a lot of battles. Some of them were against the Crusaders. Others were against enemy tribes. We lost some battles and we won many others. The battles were hard. We lost many good men, but we also conquered a lot of land.

We could never rest because we always had to prepare for new attacks. More men joined my army and I trained them well. I took control of Egypt, Libya, Palestine, Yemen, Gaza, Damascus and Syria. I also became a Sultan. The Muslim empire grew into a very big empire.

I wanted to conquer Jerusalem – to take it from the Crusaders. But the Crusaders were our worst enemy – they were very strong and they had a very big army. I decided to attack the Crusaders at the Battle of Hattin in 1187. We won the battle and we took control of Jerusalem. I ended 88 years of Crusader control of our land!

◆ ◆ ◆

But four years later, the Third Crusade arrived. The leader was King Richard the First of England. His army was strong and he won the Battle of Arsuf against us. The King's horse was killed, so I sent him two horses. I also sent him a doctor because he was <u>injured</u> in battle. The people were surprised – I was a good man.

Then we fought another battle and my army won this time. In 1192, I made peace with King Richard because we wanted to stop the war. We made an <u>agreement</u>. Muslims controlled the city of Jerusalem and Christians could come to visit it.

I decided to go back to Damascus because I was ill and my job was done. We had control of our land. On my way, I thought about my life. I asked myself, 'Will the Crusaders come back?' And my answer was, 'They will come back. There will be more wars.' It was so sad. I <u>prayed</u> for peace. In 1193, I was 56 years old when I died.

The Life of Saladin

1137   Saladin was born in Tikrit in Iraq. He was the son of a rich Muslim leader. When he was a child, he lived in Syria.

1163   He joined his uncle, Shirkuh when he invaded Egypt.

1169   Shirkuh became the new leader of Egypt. Shirkuh died and Saladin became Egypt's leader. He also became the leader of the army.

1174   Saladin conquered Damascus. He became the Sultan of Egypt, Syria, Nubia and Yemen.

1175   Syrian leader, Rashideddin, and his men tried to kill Saladin.

1176   Saladin married Ismat ad-Din Khatun.

1183   Saladin conquered the city of Aleppo in Syria. He became the best leader in the Muslim world.

1186   He won Mosul, a city in the north of Iraq from the Crusaders.

1187   He won the Battle of Hattin. He won Jerusalem from the Crusaders.

1189 The Third Crusade began. King Phillip Augustus of France, King Richard the First of England and the German Emperor, Frederick Barbarossa, were its leaders. They wanted to conquer the city of Jerusalem. Later, Frederick Barbarossa died and King Phillip Augustus returned to France.

1191 Richard the First of England fought the Battle of Arsuf against Saladin. Richard the First won the battle and took control of the city of Acre.

1192 Saladin and King Richard made an agreement called The Treaty of Ramla. Muslims controlled the city of Jerusalem, but Christians could visit it. Saladin became ill.

1193 Saladin died in Damascus, Syria. He was 56 years old.

Genghis Khan

◆ ◆ ◆

*c.*1155–1227

the leader of the Mongolian empire

When I was born, my parents called me Temujin. But later in my life, my <u>tribe</u> changed my name to Genghis Khan. My new name meant '<u>universal</u> <u>ruler</u>'. It was a good name for a man who <u>conquered</u> so much land.

♦ ◆ ♦

I was born in Asia around the year 1155. We were a Mongolian tribe and our life was very hard because we lived in desert land. We were nomads — we moved from place to place to find food and water. We also fought for land and stole animals from other tribes.

When I was a child, my father was the leader of our tribe. He was a soldier and he <u>trained</u> me for war. You had to be a good soldier to stay <u>alive</u> in our times. My mother gave me hard jobs. She asked me to cut wood and carry heavy things from one place to another. In the Mongolian Khentii Mountains, winters were very long and cold, and summers were very hot and dry. Both my parents and the mountains helped me to grow into a strong man.

◆ ◆ ◆

When I was 9 years old, my father took me to the Onggirat tribe to <u>arrange</u> my <u>marriage</u> with a young girl named Borte. On our way back home, we were attacked by the Tatars, an enemy tribe, and my father died. I was very young to become a leader, so my tribe chose another man. Now my family didn't have a tribe. We became very poor and I tried to help my mother. But our <u>situation</u> was very bad. Things didn't get better when my mother decided to marry a man who had sons. One day, I had a fight with one of my half-brothers and he died.

When I was 16 years old, I married Borte and our two tribes <u>united</u>. I was a strong soldier and I wanted to protect my family and my tribe. We hoped for times of <u>peace</u>, but soon we were attacked by the Merkit tribe. They killed many of our people and also took my wife. I was able to escape and I decided to take <u>revenge</u>. I planned our attack very carefully. I was so angry that I ordered my soldiers to kill every Merkit man. Our attack was successful and I <u>freed</u> my wife.

Borte and I had a good family life and we had four sons. But life was not easy for us because our enemies were always watching and waiting to attack. When I was about 20 years old, I was <u>captured</u> by the Tayichi'ud tribe and while I was their prisoner, they <u>beat</u> me and I had a very bad time. When I finally escaped, I said to myself, 'This time my revenge will be bigger than ever.' I had to plan a terrible attack.

I decided to take my time to plan my revenge more carefully than before. I needed a large <u>army</u> so I united my army with the army of another big tribe. Their leader was Ong Khan, a very <u>powerful</u> man. I now had an army of 20,000 men. But I needed more than a large number of men. I needed the strongest men of all. So I trained them to be strong. Our task was to <u>eliminate</u> all the other tribes.

First, in 1196, we attacked the Tatars, the tribe that killed my father. I ordered my soldiers to kill every man in their tribe. Next, we attacked the Tayichi'ud tribe. Then we moved on to attack the Naiman tribe.

Soon I had <u>control</u> over a large part of Mongolia. I had a lot of land and more power than ever before. My army was so big that I needed new ways to fight enemy tribes. I sent <u>spies</u> to get information and then, when the <u>battle</u> started, we used drums and smoke <u>signals</u> to communicate with one another.

My new idea worked really well. We won every battle. Several tribes united with us because they wanted to be on our side. My army grew to more than 80,000 men. My soldiers were very good at riding horses and they had the best <u>weapons</u>. Very often, when other tribes heard us coming, they didn't fight. They chose to unite with our tribe because they knew that we killed every man from an enemy tribe. My people thought I was the God of the Mongol people and called me 'Genghis Khan'.

Then problems started. My tribe was very big and we had very little food. I needed to conquer more land outside Mongolia. We moved on and asked other tribes to join us. But some of these tribes didn't want to join us because their <u>culture</u> was very different from our culture. They didn't want to become a Mongolian tribe. So we attacked them and killed them all. I conquered a lot of <u>Muslim</u> and Chinese lands. I also conquered the central part of Asia and took control of <u>trade routes</u> from China to Europe. My army had about 200,000 men now!

During my life, I not only fought but I also worked hard to look after my tribe. I asked my people to write our <u>law</u>. People shouldn't steal animals or sell women. People who broke the law should die. I was a great ruler and trained my sons to be great soldiers. 'Be prepared', I told them. 'Attack the enemy before they know you are there. The future of my <u>empire</u> <u>depends on</u> you.' When I died in 1227, my empire was nearly 24 million square kilometres.

Genghis Khan's empire

Legend:
- Original area of control
- Movements of Genghis Khan and his generals
- Genghis Khan's empire in 1207
- Genghis Khan's empire in 1227

0   1000 km

Tayichi'ud Tribe
Tatar Tribe
Merkit Tribe
Naiman Tribe
Beijing
Baghdad
Kiev

The Life of Genghis Khan

*c.*1155   Temujin was born in the Mongolian Khentii Mountains.

*c.*1164   His father arranged a marriage between Temujin and Borte. He was 9 years old.

*c.*1164–1165   Temujin's father was killed when he was returning from a visit to Borte's tribe. Temujin's tribe chose a new leader. Temujin and his family lost their tribe.

*c.*1171   Temujin married Borte to join two tribes. He was 16 years old. Temujin's tribe was attacked by the Merkit tribe. They took his wife. Temujin freed her. Borte had her first son.

*c.*1177   The Tayichi'ud tribe captured Temujin. He became their prisoner, but he was able to escape. He returned to form an army. Borte and Temujin had three more sons.

1196   Temujin took revenge for his father's death and attacked the Tatar tribe. Then he attacked the Tayichi'ud tribe.

1206   Temujin was given the name 'Genghis Khan'. It meant 'universal ruler'. He became the leader of the Mongolian Empire.

1211   He invaded the north of China. The war
       lasted nearly 20 years. He was interested in
       China's rice fields.

1218   He sent people from his tribe to meet
       Muslim leaders. His people were killed. He
       decided to take revenge on their leader, Shah
       Muhammad.

1219   He attacked Shah Muhammad's army. He
       killed every human and animal in the cities
       that he invaded.

1227   Genghis Khan died. His empire was
       very big. It was nearly 24 million square
       kilometres.

Catherine the Great

❖ ❖ ❖

1729–1796

the woman who turned Russia into an empire

I was not Russian, I did not speak Russian and I did not belong to the Russian Orthodox Church. I also had the wrong name. But I became the <u>Empress</u> of Russia and <u>ruled</u> the country for more than 30 years.

◆ ◆ ◆

I was called Sophia Friederike Auguste when I was born in 1729. I was 16 years old when I got married to my cousin, Peter, the <u>heir</u> to the Russian <u>throne</u>. My <u>marriage</u> was <u>arranged</u> by Elizabeth, the Empress of Russia.

The Empress was a strong woman who ruled Russia alone. She wasn't married and she didn't have any children, so she decided to find an heir to the throne. She chose her nephew, Peter, as heir and she chose me as his wife. We got married in St Petersburg on 21ˢᵗ August 1745.

After the ceremony, there was a very big party. Everyone celebrated and I thought, 'Is there a true reason to celebrate?'

I didn't love my husband and he didn't love me either. I didn't speak his language, so we couldn't talk to each other. I was born in Stettin, Prussia, and I spoke German. I didn't know a word of Russian. Our marriage was unhappy because we weren't interested in each other.

Soon the Empress started to worry. Her plans weren't working well. She wanted us to have a child – a new heir to the throne. But soon, I had a beautiful baby son. His name was Paul.

◆ ◆ ◆

The next years were a sad and difficult time for me. My baby was taken from me and the Empress didn't let me see him very often. She wanted to take care of the boy and decide on his education. She wanted to have everything under control.

I was very upset. I knew that I had to understand Russian to be able to compete with the Empress. I started to study day after day and night after night. I also needed to change my Protestant religion. I changed my name from Sophia to Catherine and I joined the Russian Orthodox Church. I grew into a strong woman myself.

When the Empress finally died in 1762, my husband became Peter the Third, Tsar of Russia. But this was not good news for me. I was worried about my future. My husband might kill me or put me in prison. He wasn't interested in me.

I thought about the Empress. When she had a problem, she made a plan. So I made a plan with Prince Gregory Orlov, a man from the <u>army</u> with <u>powerful</u> friends. Soon Orlov and his men put my husband in prison and then killed him. I lied to the people. They thought that my husband died from a stomach illness.

◆ ◆ ◆

On 22nd September 1762, I became the new Empress of Russia. I was 33 years old. I was a young woman with a lot of power. Prince Orlov asked me to marry him, but I didn't love him. And I didn't need a husband. I wanted to become a great <u>ruler</u> of Russia.

I was interested in art and education. I opened many schools and St Petersburg became a centre of <u>culture</u>. I was able to solve every problem I had. When there was danger of a war in Russia because the <u>noblemen</u> didn't like my new ideas, I gave orders to kill their leader. When our <u>borders</u> were in danger, I ordered the army to <u>conquer</u> new lands. Ukraine, Lithuania, Latvia, Belarus, Crimea and Poland became part of Russia. The country became a big <u>empire</u>.

I didn't rule Russia alone. In 1774, Grigory Potyomkin became my <u>adviser</u>. For 17 years, he helped me to make decisions and he was the leader of the army. I also got help from a lot of other people. People were happy to help me because when I asked for a favour, I always gave something <u>in return</u>.

I was the Empress of Russia for 34 years. I improved the living conditions in my country and turned it into a big empire. I was a great ruler.

I changed my name from Sophia to Catherine. Then people changed it to Catherine the Great.

Catherine the Great's empire by 1796

The Life of Catherine the Great

1729   Sophia Friederike Auguste was born in Stettin, Prussia (now Poland). When she was a child, she studied languages, religion, history and music.

1745   She got married to her cousin, Peter, the future Tsar of Russia. It was an arranged marriage. She was 16 years old.

1754   She had a son, Paul.

1757   She had a daughter, Anna.

1762   Empress Elizabeth died. Her son became Peter the Third, Tsar of Russia. He was killed. Catherine became Catherine the Second, Empress of Russia.

1764   Catherine started to collect paintings. She started The Hermitage Museum. Today it is the museum with the largest number of paintings in the world.

1767   Catherine wrote a document called the *Nakaz* about the law in Russia.

1768   She sent an army to the Polish King, Stanislaw, to help him to fight his enemies in Poland.

1770 Russia started to conquer lands. Grigory
      Potyomkin was the leader of her army.

1773 Catherine started to improve the living
      conditions in Russia. She also showed
      interest in schools and education.

1774 Grigory Potyomkin became her adviser.

1780 Russia conquered more lands.

1786 Catherine opened elementary and secondary
      schools.

1796 She died in her palace in St Petersburg,
      Russia. She was 67 years old. Her son, Paul,
      became the new Tsar.

Abraham Lincoln

◆ ◆ ◆

1809–1865

the United States President who stopped slavery

I was born in a one-room house and had very little education as a child. To educate myself, I read *The Life of George Washington, The Bible* and plays by Shakespeare. I became president of the USA and <u>freed</u> more than 3,000,000 <u>slaves</u>.

♦ ♦ ♦

I lived with my parents on a farm in the <u>state</u> of Kentucky. Our house was a small cabin with one room. My parents had little education but taught me some of the most important things in life. Respect and <u>justice</u> were always <u>valued</u> in my house.

I was a child when I learnt that life was hard. I worked on my father's farm in both good and bad weather. When I was 9 years old, my mother became ill and died. Soon my father began to have problems with the farm because he couldn't <u>compete</u> with the other farmers in the area. They owned slaves who worked for them, but my father did not. He thought that it was wrong to own slaves and that every man should be free.

My father decided to start a new life and he got married to Sarah Bush Johnston. It was the start of a new life for me, too. I became closer to Sarah than to my father. She was kind to me and she became a good <u>stepmother</u>.

◆ ◆ ◆

When I was a young man, I decided to find a job. I went on a boat down the Sangamon River and I got a job in New Salem in Illinois. My job was to take things down the river to New Orleans and sell them there. This was a great experience. I learnt to communicate with people.

Then the Black Hawk War started. It was a war against the Indians and I joined the <u>army</u>. This was another important experience in my life. 'There must be a better way of solving problems,' I thought.

After the war, I decided to educate myself. I read *The Life of George Washington*, *The Bible* and plays by Shakespeare. I was interested in the <u>law</u> and politics and these books helped me develop my ideas. I also opened a shop in New Salem because I needed to make some money while I studied.

When I became a lawyer in 1837, I stopped working in the store, and I started an office with William Herndon, a lawyer who was against <u>slavery</u>. I thought that the only way to stop slavery was with political <u>action</u>, so I decided to begin my political career. I began to work for the Illinois State Legislature. In a legislature, laws are decided. I thought that life should be fair for everyone and it was necessary to have the right laws.

When I became leader of the Illinois Whig Party, I began to explain my views in public. I said that I wanted 'a government of the people, for the people and by the people.' I also said that slavery was not fair.

A lot of people didn't share my views. One of them was my fiancée's father, Mr Todd. He was a rich man who had a lot of slaves. However, Mary and I got married and later had four sons.

◆ ◆ ◆

In 1846, I was <u>elected</u> to the United States Congress. In Congress, people make the country's laws.

In 1847, I started work as a lawyer again. It was a useful time because I talked to a lot of people and I learnt about their problems. Then in 1856, I joined the Republican Party and became its leader until in 1860, I won an election and became President.

It wasn't easy. When I became President, seven southern states decided to form a new country, the Confederate States of America. The people who lived in these states had slaves. They didn't want me as President because I wanted to stop slavery.

On 12th April 1861, I <u>declared</u> war. I wanted to join the north with the south into one country again and the

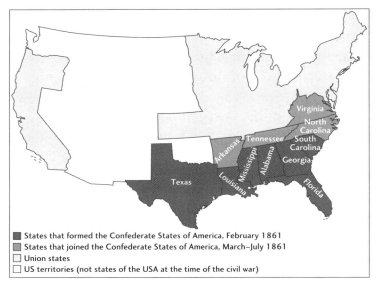

The Confederate States of America in 1861

American Civil War began. It was a sad time for all of us. Two years later, I declared that more than 3,000,000 people were free from slavery. Now white people had to pay black people for their work. Many of them didn't want to pay them, but they had to respect the law.

In 1864, I started my second term as President of the United States. The war continued until 9th April 1865. We paid a terrible price for the war. 600,000 Americans died. And the war also cost my life. One day, I was at the theatre with my wife when I was shot and killed by John Wilkes Booth. He ended my Presidency, but he did not end my cause. I died, but the country was one country again and slaves were already free.

The Life of Abraham Lincoln

1809 Abraham Lincoln was born in Kentucky, USA.

1818 His mother died when he was 9 years old.

1819 His father married Sarah Bush Johnston.

1828 He worked on a boat that sailed to New Orleans.

1830 His family moved to Illinois.

1831 He went on a boat for a second time. He worked in a shop in New Salem, Illinois.

1832 He joined the army during the Black Hawk War. He opened a shop with his friend William Berry.

1834 He began to study law.

1835 He became a leader of the Whig Party.

1842 He got married to Mary Todd. They later had four sons.

1844–1845 He worked as a lawyer.

1846 He was elected to the United States Congress. In Congress, people make the country's laws.

1847–1849   He left politics to work as a lawyer again.

1854   He gave his views against slavery in public.

1856   He helped to form the new Republican Party.

1860   He was elected as the 16th President of the United States.

1861   The American Civil War began. The war lasted until 1865. The Confederate States of America was formed.

1863   He freed more than 3,000,000 slaves.

1864   He was elected President again.

1865   On 14th April, he was shot in the head. He died the next day. He was 56 years old. By the end of the year, all slaves were declared free.

Queen
Victoria

◆ ◆

1819–1901

the Queen who gave her name to the Victorian Age

I was one of the most famous queens in the world and I gave my name to the Victorian <u>Age</u>. But when I became Queen of England, I didn't want to be Queen. I was very young.

◆ ◆ ◆

I was born in London on 24th May 1819. I was the only child of Edward, Duke of Kent, and Princess Victoria Mary Louise of Saxe-Coburg. I became Queen when my uncle William the Fourth died in 1837. I didn't want to become a queen. I was 18 years old and I wanted to have a good time. Also, although I was educated in England, I felt more German than English. I spoke German because my mother was from Germany and she spoke to me in her language. My father was from England but he died when I was only 8 months old.

As soon as I became Queen, I learnt that I had a lot of <u>responsibilities</u> but no power at all. From the beginning, Lord Melbourne, the <u>Prime Minister</u>, told me, 'Politics are not for kings or queens. They're for politicians.'

'I have to change this,' I thought. 'I'm the Queen of England and Scotland, and I want to make decisions. I want to choose the people who will work for me.' Soon several wives of politicians were working for me.

In 1836, I met my German cousin Albert of Saxe-Coburg and Gotha, and we got married four years later. Our <u>marriage</u> was <u>arranged</u> for us, but we loved each other. We could communicate easily because I could speak his language and we got on really well. He gave me good advice on money matters and we took decisions together. We worked as a team.

Our problem was that we were very unpopular. I wasn't popular among politicians because I wanted to <u>rule</u> and make decisions. And my husband wasn't popular among the people because he wasn't British. We soon found out that we had a lot of enemies.

People tried to kill us several times. One day, my husband and I were travelling on a <u>coach</u> when a man shot at us. His <u>bullets</u> didn't hit us, so we were not hurt. Two years later, the same thing happened again. Then one day, another man tried to kill us, but luckily, he didn't have any bullets in his gun. 'This is a dangerous job,' I thought.

◆ ◆ ◆

At the beginning of my <u>reign</u>, life for British people was very hard. In Ireland, thousands of people died because they had no food. In London, a lot of people didn't have a job and there were a lot of <u>beggars</u> in the streets.

I ruled during the <u>Industrial Revolution</u>. It was a time of technological advances. Factories started using new machines and the world's first trains started carrying things from one place to another. Cities grew fast because people moved from the countryside to the city to find jobs in factories. But factory workers earned very little money and they couldn't buy a place to live, so they lived in very bad conditions in old buildings.

I lived in Buckingham Palace. It was a beautiful building in London. I enjoyed a happy family life with my husband and our nine children – five daughters and four sons. But our palace wasn't only a home. It was an important meeting place, too. Many kings and leaders from other countries came to visit us. They liked the beautiful building and the paintings on its walls.

Another important building in my time was Crystal Palace. It was in London, too. It was a very large building made of glass. In 1851, there was a Great <u>Exhibition</u> at Crystal Palace. People from all over the world came to see the new inventions and machines that were shown there. My husband and I often went to the exhibition to meet the visitors. We enjoyed our public life.

◆ ◆ ◆

But one day in 1861, when I was 42 years old, Albert became ill and soon died. I never recovered from his death. I was the mother of nine children and the <u>ruler</u> of a big country. I had a lot of responsibilities. My servants – the people who worked for me – and government <u>officials</u> tried to help me, but life was very difficult. I decided to stop my public life.

During my reign, Britain became the most <u>powerful</u> country in the world. The British <u>Empire</u> grew and became the biggest empire in history. It included India, Australia, Canada and South Africa. There was much more <u>trade</u>. There were more jobs for the people and living conditions were better for everyone.

◆ ◆ ◆

I never visited any of the <u>colonies</u> of the British Empire, but I travelled to Scotland several times. I had a friend there and I liked to talk about my problems with him. His name was John Brown. People didn't like my visits to Scotland because they thought that I spent too much time there. I knew that I wasn't a popular Queen. I also knew that my visits to Scotland were not helping me to become popular. But one day, when I was coming back from one of my visits, a man tried to kill me. To my surprise, people were sorry for me. I became a popular Queen! And later, when the country celebrated my reign of 50 and then 60 years, people were very happy and showed a lot of respect for me.

I kept a diary during my life. I wrote about 2,500 words a day. My notes helped me to think and make the right decisions. I wanted to help my people and I did a good job. I ruled my country for 63 years and seven months, and I gave my name to a period of history – the Victorian Age.

The Life of Queen Victoria

1819 Princess Alexandrina Victoria was born at Kensington Palace on 24th May. She was the only child of Edward, Duke of Kent, and Princess Victoria Mary Louise of Saxe-Coburg-Saalfeld.

1820 When her father died in January, she became heir to the English throne. She was only 8 months old.

1837 On 20th June, King William the Fourth died and Victoria became Queen.

1839 She became engaged to be married to her first cousin, Prince Albert.

1840 Victoria and Albert married on 10th January at the Chapel Royal in St James' Palace. They had their first child, Victoria. A man tried to kill them.

1841 She had her second child, Albert Edward.

1842 Twice this year, people tried to kill her. She travelled to London by train for the first time.

1843–1850 Her children Alice, Alfred, Helena, Louise and Arthur were born.

1851	There was a Great Exhibition at Crystal Palace in London. Albert and Victoria were often there. The exhibition was about art, science, trade and industry.
1853–1857	Leopold and Beatrice were born.
1861	Her husband died. Victoria stopped her public life and wore black for the rest of her life.
1877	She was given the title of Empress of India.
1882	A man tried to kill her. It was the seventh time someone tried to kill her. It was the last one, too.
1887	The country celebrated 50 years of Victoria's reign.
1897	The country celebrated 60 years of Victoria's reign. Britain was the most powerful country in the world.
1901	Victoria died in Osborne House on the Isle of Wight. She was 81 years old. Her reign became known as the Victorian Age.

◆ Glossary ◆

action UNCOUNTABLE NOUN
when you do something for a
particular purpose

adviser NOUN
an expert whose job is to give
advice

age NOUN
a period in history

agreement NOUN
a plan or a decision that two or
more people have made

alive ADJECTIVE
living, not dead

army NOUN
a large group of soldiers who are
trained to fight battles on land

arrange VERB
to make plans for an event to
happen

baron NOUN
a man who has a title and is of a
high social rank

battle NOUN
a violent fight between groups of
people, especially between
armies during a war

**beat (beats, beating, beat,
beaten)** VERB
to hit someone very hard

beggar NOUN
someone who lives by asking
people for money or food

border NOUN
an imaginary line that divides two
countries

bullet NOUN
a small piece of metal that is shot
out of a gun

capture VERB
to catch someone and keep them
somewhere so that they cannot
leave

cause NOUN
an aim that some people support
or fight for

ceremony NOUN
a formal event such as a wedding

coach NOUN
a vehicle with four wheels that is
pulled by horses

colony NOUN
an area that is controlled by
another country

compete VERB
to try to be better than someone
or to get something that they
also want to have

conquer VERB
to take complete control of the
land of another country or group
of people

control UNCOUNTABLE NOUN
the power to make all the
important decisions about
something

Crusade NOUN
one of the wars between
Christians and Muslims that were
fought in Palestine during the
11th, 12th and 13th centuries

Crusader NOUN
a soldier who fought in the
Crusades

culture NOUN
the way of life, the traditions and
the beliefs of a particular group
of people

declare VERB
to officially state that something
is the case

depend on PHRASAL VERB
to need someone or something
in order to do something

destroy VERB
to cause so much damage to
something that it cannot be used
any longer, or does not exist any
longer

elect VERB
to choose a person to do a
particular job by voting for them

eliminate VERB
to kill an enemy

empire NOUN
a number of separate nations
that are all controlled by the
ruler of one particular country

empress NOUN
a woman who rules an empire, or
the wife of an emperor

exhibition NOUN
a public event where art or
interesting objects are shown

free VERB
to release a prisoner or slave

heir NOUN
someone who will receive a
person's money, property or title
when that person dies

Industrial Revolution NOUN
the period in history during
which machines started to be
used to make things

injured ADJECTIVE
having suffered damage to part
of the body

invade VERB
to attack and enter a country

invader NOUN
a soldier or an army that enters a
country in order to attack it

justice UNCOUNTABLE NOUN
the fair treatment of people

law NOUN
an official rule that the people of
a country must obey

march VERB
to walk somewhere with regular
steps, as a group

marriage NOUN
the relationship between a
husband and a wife
the time when two people get
married

Muslim NOUN
someone who believes in the
religion of Islam and lives
according to its rules

nobleman (noblemen) NOUN
in former times, a man of a high
social rank who had a title

official NOUN
a person who holds a position of
power in an organization

peace UNCOUNTABLE NOUN
a situation where there is not
a war

port NOUN
a town by the sea where ships
arrive and leave

powerful ADJECTIVE
able to control people and
events

pray VERB
to speak to God or a god

priest NOUN
a person who has religious duties
in a place where people worship

Prime Minister NOUN
the leader of the government in
some countries

Protestant ADJECTIVE
belonging to the part of the
Christian church that is not the
Catholic church

rebellion NOUN
a situation in which a large group of people fight against the people who are in charge, for example, the government

reign NOUN
the period of time during which someone is king or queen

responsibility NOUN
a duty

return
in return done because someone did something for you

revenge UNCOUNTABLE NOUN
something bad you do to someone who has hurt or harmed you

rule VERB
to control the affairs of a country

ruler NOUN
the person who rules a country

signal NOUN
a movement, a light or a sound that gives a particular message to the person who sees or hears it

situation NOUN
what is happening in a particular place at a particular time

slave NOUN
a person who belongs to another person and who works for them without being paid

slavery UNCOUNTABLE NOUN
the system by which people are owned by other people as slaves

spy NOUN
a person whose job is to find out secret information about another country or organization

state NOUN
a smaller area that some large countries such as the United States are divided into

stepmother NOUN
the woman who has married someone's father but who is not their mother

throne NOUN
the position of being king or queen

trade UNCOUNTABLE NOUN
the buying and selling of goods

trade route NOUN
a way of getting from one place to another, used mainly by people travelling long distances to buy and sell goods

train VERB
to teach someone the skills that they need in order to do something

tribe NOUN
a group of people of the same race, language and culture, especially in a developing country

unite VERB
to join together and act as a group

universal ADJECTIVE
including or affecting everyone

value VERB
to think that something or someone is important

weapon NOUN
an object such as a gun, that is used for killing or hurting people

Collins
English Readers

AMAZING PEOPLE READERS AT OTHER LEVELS:

Level 2

Amazing Aviators
978-0-00-754495-0

Amazing Architects and Artists
978-0-00-754496-7

Amazing Composers *(May 2014)*
978-0-00-754502-5

Amazing Mathematicians
(May 2014)
978-0-00-754503-2

Amazing Medical People
(June 2014)
978-0-00-754509-4

Level 3

Amazing Explorers
978-0-00-754497-4

Amazing Writers
978-0-00-754498-1

Amazing Philanthropists
(May 2014)
978-0-00-754504-9

Amazing Performers
(May 2014)
978-0-00-754505-6

Amazing Scientists *(June 2014)*
978-0-00-754510-0

Level 4

Amazing Thinkers and Humanitarians
978-0-00-754499-8

Amazing Scientists
978-0-00-754500-1

Amazing Writers *(May 2014)*
978-0-00-754506-3

Amazing Leaders *(May 2014)*
978-0-00-754507-0

Amazing Entrepreneurs and Business People *(June 2014)*
978-0-00-754511-7

Visit **www.collinselt.com/readers** for language activities, teacher's notes, and to find out more about the series.

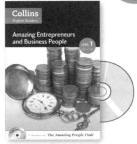